A HANDBOOK FOR READERS

A Practical and Liturgical Guide

Marian Tolley

Decani Books

First published in 2001 by Decani Books, 30 North Terrace, Mildenhall, Suffolk IP28 7AB

© 2001 Marian Tolley
Cover photographs by Tegwyn Roberts

ISBN 1 900314 12 6

Printed by RPM Reprographics (Chichester) Ltd, Units 2-3 Spur Road, Quarry Lane, Chichester, West Sussex, PO19 2PR

Acknowledgements

I take this opportunity to thank some of the people who have been guides and mentors, sharing their love of the liturgy and providing encouragement when it was needed –

Canon Laurence Pelosi, who first enabled and encouraged and guided,
Bishop Edwin, whose support made it possible to learn through teaching,
Sue and Stephen, who have a gift for persuading many to give more than they think they're ready for,
Rod, who is indispensable and who has always helped clear the way,
and my fellow parishioners at St Winefride's in Welshpool and St Garmon's in Llanfechain, who have been my faith family, with whom I have learned so much -

and for the gift of friendship and support from others unnamed, my debt is hereby gratefully acknowledged.

CONTENTS

Foreword

FOR THE PAST FIVE YEARS, the Liturgy Commission of the Diocese of Wrexham has continued working towards the vision of Church expressed in the documents of Vatican II. Among the achievements so far has been the conduct of a course in Basic Liturgical Formation for the whole Diocese, and the celebration of the Jubilee Mass in Llangollen in 2000. The Diocesan Congress in autumn 2000 gave us a vision of the kind of Church the Spirit is calling us to be.

At the heart of these and related activities is an awareness of the importance of liturgy as the engine of all that we do. The lead in renewing an understanding of the reformed liturgy and in fostering and introducing better practices has been, and continues to be, the responsibility of the Liturgy Commission. This handbook,written by one of the members, is an example of the knowledge and experience that has been gained.

While I am aware that the understanding of this ministry and the recommendations put forward in the work which follows were gained in this Diocese, I am sure that it will benefit all who read it, whether as individuals, as groups of readers in a parish, or indeed as persons who simply wish to be better informed about the Liturgy of the Word.

I am pleased to recommend this work and hope all who make use of it will be helped to hear the Word of the Lord better.

✠ **Edwin Regan**
Bishop of Wrexham

Introduction

T HIS IS A HANDBOOK FOR READERS, which means its purpose is to give positive guidance on all aspects, practical and spiritual, of doing this ministry well.

The natural expectation of such a book is that it would contain specific recommendations for preparation and conduct during the reading.

However, the source of the Church's understanding of this ministry, the General Introduction to the Lectionary, is so important, clear and inviting and yet has been so neglected by those responsible for the celebration of the liturgy that the first main section of this handbook will focus on this document.

Following this, the emphasis moves on to the practical aspects, and the handbook closes with a consideration of ministry.

I. In the beginning

How did the ministry of reading begin for you? Think back to the beginning of your experience with this role and see if what follows is similar to your memories.

The original request was probably from the person who made up the readers' rota, who asked if you would be willing to read at Sunday Mass. It is slightly less likely that you were asked by the parish priest, or that you might have volunteered for the job. Once agreement was reached, however, you worked out what you were supposed to do with not too much help from anyone. You modeled your demeanour and approach on what others were already doing, choosing to imitate what seemed to you to be the best models. It is not likely that anyone talked to you about what being a reader is about or how to do it. The quality which seemed to be most useful was courage.

For preparation, you worked on your own a few days before, either reading from your missal or, if your parish uses them, a copy of the relevant missalette or Parish Mass Book. Sometimes you wouldn't remember when you were supposed to read and only prepare it on the very day.

On the Sunday of your reading, you would go forward to the front, but perhaps you stood beside the lectern, not at it, and perhaps you brought with you the missal or missalette you had used during your preparation because you were familiar with it and felt comfortable with it.

On the day, as only one reader was scheduled for each Sunday, you were expected to do both readings, the psalm in between them, and the Gospel Acclamation. You might have introduced them by saying 'The first reading is...', 'The response to the Responsorial Psalm is...', 'The second reading is a reading from...', 'All rise for the Gospel Acclamation'.

If you received any feedback from the congregation, it was probably complimentary and brief. But is unlikely that anyone made any specific suggestions about how you might improve your reading.

At some time, after you had been reading for a while, you began to wonder if you were doing the right thing, if you were doing enough, if there was a way to improve. This might have been especially the case if you noticed the way in which Extraordinary Ministers of the Eucharist seemed to be taken so much more seriously, being not only trained, but commissioned for their ministry.

Doing better

So, we arrive at the point where we want to know more in order to do better.

Before continuing to suggest ways in which this can happen, it is important to point out that the imaginary scenario just outlined is not meant as criticism. This is probably the way most of us began, and there are positive things that should be said about it.

Firstly, by agreeing to read Scripture in the Church, you have demonstrated one of the great strengths of the modern Catholic Church: the *willingness of lay people* to take a full part in the liturgy which we celebrate together. Without this foundation, there would be no point in going further.

Secondly, there is no question that when you began, you did *the best you could*, given what you knew at the time. No one accepts the responsibility of becoming a reader intending to do it poorly. It is important to acknowledge how much good practice has already become established since this ministry became a feature of church life in the 1960s. But, although our intentions are the best, it is absolutely the case that when we know better, we can do better. And there is always room for improvement.

So, no criticism is intended in pointing out that there is a gap between the way that most of us began this ministry of reading and the information, understanding and skills needed for us to improve the way in which we fulfill our role as readers.

Where do we go if we want to find out what the expectations of this ministry really are: if we want guidance about what we should do?

The Bible and the Lectionary

Before we begin, it is important when discussing scripture to understand clearly the distinction between the Bible and the Lectionary.

Bible

The Bible is one of the greatest treasures we have. Although contained in one volume, it is a collection of 73 different works by different authors, using different styles and perspectives, which was written over several centuries in Hebrew and Greek, with maybe some of the New Testament beginning life in Aramaic. The writings were gradually collected and went through a process of editing and tidying up. Nevertheless we have a richness and diversity and you will often find the same story told at different times, from different perspectives, by different authors, for different audiences.

Underlying all the writing, however, is the authors' shared conviction that 'God's presence is felt in human history and that God invites the human family to respond with faith and integrity'.* After thinking about events in the history of Israel, in the life and death of Jesus and in the experiences of the early church, the biblical authors, under the inspiration of the Holy Spirit, wrote to make clear the presence of God in the remembered events. They look at the stories they relate through the eyes of faith. They are

---

The Catholic Bible, ed J.M. Hiesberger, OUP, 1995, p 1

the foundation of the Church's knowledge and faith too, because we, like the original hearers, are convinced of the power of these writings which come from the presence of God in them: a presence which the General Instruction on the Roman Missal (a document which will be referred to again later) has strongly affirmed:

> When the scriptures are read in Church, God himself is speaking to his people, and Christ, present in his own word, is proclaiming the Gospel. (9; 2000 edition, 29)

The question of this 'presence' will be returned to several times during this book. It parallels the 'real presence' of the Eucharist. This means that not only Eucharistic ministers but Readers as well are handling holy things, which shows how seriously this ministry should be taken.

Lectionary

The Lectionary which is used during liturgical celebrations today is an ordered system of selected readings from the Bible.

The practice of choosing extracts from the books of the Bible began in the synagogue and was carried forward in the early Church. Over the centuries each branch of the Church developed its own Lectionary cycle of readings. Up until 1969 our part of it, the Roman Rite, had a cycle which only included two readings on a Sunday, with the Old Testament rarely being read, and which was repeated each year instead of every third year as now. Then came the great reform of the Catholic Church begun by Pope John XXIII. There were many reforms at Vatican II but one of the main ones, less often referred to, is the new Lectionary. The Council had determined to widen the choice available for readings on Sundays. The Constitution on the Sacred Liturgy, in which the Council's liturgical reforms are set out, said:

> The treasures of the Bible are to be opened up more lavishly, so that a richer share in God's word may be provided for the faithful. In this way a more representative portion of holy Scripture will be read to the people in the course of the prescribed number of years. (CSL51)

This resulted in the creation of a 3-year cycle for Sundays and a 2-year cycle for weekdays. The new Lectionary is one of the foundations of the great reform. Together with the Sacramentary (the book, used by the presider, containing the prayers of the Mass), it forms part of the Roman Missal.

The new Lectionary came into use on the first Sunday of Advent, 1969. In 1981 there was a second edition but it was little changed from the first, except in one important respect: the Introduction.

The Source of Guidance for the Reader

If you want to find where the Church has spoken in greatest detail about the reading of scripture in the Liturgy, the place to begin is The General Introduction to the Lectionary. This is printed at the front of the first volume of the Lectionary itself. It also appears in collections of the conciliar and post-conciliar documents of Vatican II.

The present book is a handbook for readers, which means its purpose is to give positive guidance on all aspects, practical and spiritual, of exercising this ministry well.

The refore we will begin with the General Introduction to learn what the thinking of the Church is concerning the Liturgy of the Word and the role of the reader.

II. The General Introduction to the Lectionary (GIL)

THERE IS NO SUBSTITUTE FOR READING THE INTRODUCTION YOURSELF. This would be a fairly difficult thing to do if you had to borrow the Lectionary itself, since there is usually only one Lectionary in the parish, which is kept in the church, and you are unlikely to be allowed to borrow it. However, there are easily obtainable collections of documents in which it is included.*

Since The General Introduction to the Lectionary (henceforth referred to as GIL) is indispensable in explaining the vision of the Church regarding Scripture in church services, an overview will be given, followed by highlights of the most important points for us as readers. The other foundational document of the Vatican II reforms, which forms part of the Roman Missal, also deals with the Liturgy of the Word and reference will be made to it: The General Instruction of the Roman Missal, referred to henceforth as GIRM.

The GIL consists of three main sections:

1) a **Prologue**, Chapter I, which presents and discusses the general principles of liturgical celebrations of the Word of God. It emphasises the importance of the Word of God in all celebrations of the sacraments and in the life of the Church.

2) **Part One** is concerned with the Word of God in the celebration of the Mass, outlining the elements of the Liturgy of the Word,

---

* See Documents and Further Reading, page 46.

the aids to its proper celebration (in Chapter II), and identifying the offices and ministries of those charged with responsibility for proclaiming the word (Chapter III). This is the section with most immediate significance for us as readers.

3) **Part Two** deals with the structure of the order of readings for Mass in three chapters. Chapter IV presents the general plan including the pastoral reasons for the expansion of the lectionary and covers not only Sundays and solemnities, but weekdays, saints' days and ritual masses, as well as options in the choice of some texts and the responsorial psalm and the acclamation before the Gospel. Chapter V gives a more detailed description of the Order of Readings for the liturgical seasons for both Sundays and weekdays. The final chapter covers adaptations, translations and the format for the Order of Readings. The GIL concludes with tables setting out the readings for Sundays and weekdays. Readers will find this section helpful in explaining the selections extracted from the Bible to form the Lectionary.

Having presented this overview, it is not my intention to analyse every part of GIL, but to concentrate on the sections which will be of most benefit to us as we seek to improve the way in which we conduct ourselves as readers. We begin with the section which states the expectations of those who will proclaim sacred scripture in liturgical celebrations:
- the spiritual and liturgical understanding which is expected;
- the technical skills needed; and
- what involvement in this ministry means.

This is not the order in which they appear in GIL, but they may be more accessible if dealt with in this order, especially since this is the most convenient approach to improving our reading skills.

All of this is laid out quite clearly in Chapter III on *Offices and Ministries in the Celebration of the Liturgy of the Word within Mass:*

> It is necessary that those who exercise the ministry of reader, even if they have not received institution, be truly qualified and carefully prepared so that the faithful may develop a warm

and living love for Scripture from listening to the sacred texts read.

Their preparation must above all be spiritual, but what may be called a technical preparation is also needed. The spiritual preparation presupposes at least a biblical and liturgical formation. The purpose of their biblical formation is to give readers the ability to understand the readings in context and to perceive by the light of faith the central point of the revealed message. The liturgical formation ought to equip the readers to have some grasp of the meaning and structure of the Liturgy of the Word and of the significance of its connection with the liturgy of the eucharist. The technical preparation should make the readers more skilled in the art of reading publicly, either with the power of their own voice or with the help of sound equipment.' *(55)*

Biblical Formation

This is the place where we can begin: by developing our understanding of the readings in context, and by trying in the light of faith to understand the central point of the message in the passage assigned to a particular Sunday.

A Sample Sunday

Here is an example: the 13th Sunday in Ordinary Time, Year A.

The first reading is from the second book of the Kings, 4: 8-11, 14-18. Note first that the selection prescribes only certain verses of chapter 4. To find the context we need to take a Bible (it doesn't have to be the same translation as the Jerusalem Bible used in our present Lectionary) and look at the whole of the chapter.

We find that it contains four stories: the widow's oil, Elisha and the Shunammite women (from which today's reading is drawn), the poisoned stew, and the multiplication of loaves. If you are new to this process of preparation, it may be enough on this occasion to read just the story of Elisha and the Shunammite women (verses 11 to 37). You will discover that there is much more to the story

17

than just the woman's welcome to Elisha. In fact, it paints a wonderfully vivid picture of the character and power of the prophet as well as giving a well-drawn picture of the woman. To understand the nine verses (out of twenty-seven) selected for today's reading, it greatly helps to have the whole picture contained in the longer passage. (There are other questions as well, about *content* rather than *context*: where was Shunem? Who for that matter was Elisha? Why does it matter to us in the 21st century anyway? These are questions which you can only answer by looking in a reference book: see the booklist on p.46; and see p.33 as well.)

Leaving this aside for the moment, we can still ask the general question: why was this passage chosen for this Sunday? Why take only the beginning of the story and not its dramatic and satisfying end? There are several places in GIL where the answer to these questions is to be found:

The New Testament lies hidden in the Old; the Old Testament comes fully to light in the New. (5)

The reading of the Gospel is the high point of the Liturgy of the Word. For this the other readings, in their established sequences from the Old to the New Testament, prepare the assembly. (13)

The principles governing the Order of Readings for Sundays... are called the principles of 'harmony' and of 'semi-continuous reading.' (66.3)

Harmony between First Reading and Gospel

The best instance of harmony between the Old and New Testament readings occurs when it is one that Scripture itself suggests. This is the case when the teaching and events recounted in texts of the New Testament bear a more or less explicit relationship to the teaching and events of the Old Testament. The present Order of Readings selects Old Testament texts mainly because of their correlation with New Testament texts read in the same Mass, and particularly with the Gospel text:

[For the Sundays of Ordinary Time] ... the texts of both the apostolic and Gospel readings are arranged in an order of semicontinuous reading, whereas the Old Testament reading is harmonized with the Gospel. (67)

Therefore, the reason for this shortened version of the Shunammite woman's story prescribed for this Sunday is to be found by looking at the Gospel for the day: Matthew 10:37-42. The connection seems to lie in the Gospel message that whoever welcomes a prophet welcomes Christ and will receive a prophet's reward. And thus, the reason for the choice becomes clear - by welcoming Elisha, the woman was given the unexpected gift of a son. (But we only find out what this is by reading the whole story.) It is this aspect which the compilers of the new Lectionary, who worked in Rome between the end of the Council and the publication of the Lectionary in Latin in 1968, wished to emphasise.

The **Gospel** passage from Matthew (10: 37-42) reports Jesus telling his apostles:

> Anyone who welcomes you welcomes me; and those who welcome me welcome the one who sent me. Anyone who welcomes a prophet because he is a prophet will have a prophet's reward; and anyone who welcomes a holy man because he is a holy man will have a holy man's reward. (40-41)

It is understandable that a prophet and a holy man should be rewarded; but for someone who merely receives them to be given the same reward is unexpectedly generous! The point here is that every gift we give to our neighbour out of love of God is surpassed by the abundance of God's generosity to us. If we have read the whole story of the Shunammite woman, we see proof of Matthew's point: the woman's hospitality to the prophet resulted not only in the gift of a son, but the resuscitation of that son by Elisha when the child died.

Our preparation has covered two steps which relate to Biblical formation:

– reading the *whole story* in its full scriptural context, and

– reading the *Gospel assigned for the day* in order to discover the connection between the Gospel and first reading.

19

Second Readings

If you are preparing the second reading for the 13th Sunday in Year A, you should be aware that the principle which determined the choice of Paul's letter to the Romans, 6:3-4.8-11, is not, as in the case of the first reading, harmony with the other readings. Rather it is the second principle explained in GIL paragraph 66.3 (see page 18) of *semi-continuous reading* of the apostolic writings (the letters of Paul, Peter, John, James and Jude). Paul's letters to the Romans begin on the 9th Sunday of Year A (after a series of readings from the letters to the Corinthians which began on the Second Sunday) and continues until the 25th when the choice switches to his letter to the Philippians.

It will not be surprising then if quite often there is no close relationship between the second reading and the Gospel. Some people have questioned whether this 'semi-detached' reading is a good idea, but a good homilist should be able to bring light to the situation. In favour of the system, it does counterbalance the common idea that every Mass must have a 'theme.' It is not said anywhere in the official documents that this is so. The Word of God is too big and various to be accommodated within a 'theme.' The truth rather is that *every*Mass is a celebration of the Paschal mystery of Christ's death, resurrection and ascension, and in the case of this particular Sunday the connection is made very obvious by this splendid passage of St Paul, which we also hear in the New Testament reading of the Easter Vigil.

It should be said also that the 'semi-continuous reading' principle only applies to the Sundays of Ordinary Time. During the great liturgical seasons, Advent-Christmastide, Lent-Eastertide, and on feasts like the Assumption, Ss Peter and Paul, etc., all three readings of the Mass are chosen to harmonize. Look at a Sunday in Advent or Lent to see this.

Being aware

Were you aware, as a member of the assembly, how the readings were selected? You might think that an understanding of the system might be helpful to the assembly at large and not just to the reader. Provision can be made for this in a number of ways, for example:

1) by beginning each liturgical season with an explanation of the biblical source of the readings, especially in a supplement to the Sunday bulletin;

2) by a brief summary of the readings from the presider of the day, preferably a simple sentence before the first or second reading or in the introduction to the Mass itself after the greeting.

This section on the biblical formation essential to somone preparing to be a reader can be summarised here even though the points will be repeated later when we spell out all the steps recommended for preparation. See box below:

> **Read the assigned passage**
> in its context in the Bible. See what the whole story is as presented by the author.
> **Read the key passage**
> -that is, the Gospel assigned for the day. This is the reason for the selection of the first reading and will help to make clear the point which is to be made.

If these steps of preparation are to be done well, it is obvious that the reader needs to begin early enough to get them done without haste.

A Spiritual Formation

The biblical and liturgical preparations are described in *GIL* as part of the spiritual formation necessary to the reader, but there is also a spiritual side which should imbue the whole process of preparation. While reading the assigned passage in the Lectionary, the passage in its full context in the Bible, and the Gospel for the day, the reader should also be *praying* with the text, looking out for its meaning on a personal level.

If it is true that in the biblical readings during the celebration of the Mass, 'even now, "God is speaking to his people," (*GIL* 12) then we as readers need to hear him speaking to us *individually* as we make our preparations. We must take the time to hear the message for us in the passage we are preparing or we will not be able to make our reading meaningful for the assembly.

Let it not happen that anyone in the assembly is left in doubt about the power of the reading we proclaim, indeed the very presence of God in the Word as we read (see p.12). By our preparation and by our prayer over the text, we can help to make clear God's message to those listening.

Liturgical understanding

In addition to an understanding of the biblical dimension of our ministry, we need

some grasp of the **meaning** and **structure** of the Liturgy of the Word and of the significance of its connection with the liturgy of the eucharist. (*GIL* 55, emphasis added)

This has already partly been covered in the discussion of the first and second readings and the Gospel. But there is more to the Liturgy of the Word than this - several more elements, in fact.

Besides the three prose readings, there is also the **Responsorial Psalm** - part of Scripture, of course, though people unaccountably overlook this fact when they talk about the 'three readings'. The psalm for the day is generally the one printed in the Lectionary for the Sunday (although there are some Common Psalms which can be substituted, to make it easier for people to sing rather than recite the Psalm) because

> the individual psalm texts are directly connected with the individual readings: the choice of psalm depends therefore on the readings. (*GIRM*36)

> As a rule, the responsorial psalm should be sung (*GIL* 20)

The Psalm for Sunday 13, Year A, is Psalm 89 (88) verses 2-3, 16-19, with the response *I will sing for ever of your love, O Lord.* Psalms are of different kinds, and the Psalter is a very mixed collection of songs compiled over several centuries, not written in one go by King David as once thought. *Reading* a song is a problematic thing (imagine reading a Christmas carol) and the psalm is properly the province of a Cantor. But regardless of who 'does' the psalm, the reader should look at it during preparation because it is very often the Psalm Response which gives the key to what the rest of the readings are about. Go through the readings of this Sunday with the words 'I will sing for ever of your love, O Lord' in mind and it may well make them clearer for you. And, of course, these are words which the whole assembly utters: they are its way of expressing agreement and 'ownership' of the whole Liturgy of the Word.

After the second reading and before the reading of the Gospel, there is a **Gospel Acclamation** which is an Alleluia except in Lent when it is replaced by a phrase which means basically the same thing but which reminds us of what season it is. The GIL specifies that

> the Alleluia or the verse before the Gospel must be sung (23).

> If not sung, the Alleluia or the verse before the Gospel may be omitted (*GIRM*39).

The **homily**, usually given by the presider, is an extremely important part of the Liturgy of the Word, because its purpose is to lead the community of the faithful to celebrate the eucharist wholeheartedly. Whether the homily breaks open the biblical Word of God proclaimed in the readings or some other text of the liturgy, the Church's celebration of the day's liturgy will have greater impact. (24)

The fifth element of the Liturgy of the Word is often neglected, and this is **silence**. The Introduction could not be clearer:

The Liturgy of the Word must be celebrated in a way that fosters meditation; clearly, any sort of haste that hinders reflectiveness must be avoided. The dialogue between God and his people taking place through the Holy Spirit demands short intervals of silence, suited to the assembly, as an opportunity to take the Word of God to heart and to prepare a response to it in prayer. Proper times for silence during the Liturgy of the Word are, for example, before this liturgy begins, after the first and the second reading, after the homily. (28)

Recommendations for how this can be done will be dealt with in the practical section of this handbook.

The **Profession of Faith** (Creed), proclaimed on Sundays and solemnities,

serves as a way for the people to respond and to give their assent to the Word of God heard in ths readings and through the homily and for them to call to mind the truths of faith before they begin to celebrate the eucharist. (*GIRM*43)

Prayer of the Faithful

The last part of the Liturgy of the Word is the Prayer of the Faithful or **General Intercessions**. These are one of the great potential riches of the revised post-Vatican II liturgy. Here the assembly prays for the needs of the universal church and the local community, for the salvation of the world and those oppressed by any burden, and for special categories of people. In these prayers, the people exercise their priestly function

with the result that, as the Liturgy of the Word has its full effects in them, they are better prepared to proceed to the liturgy of the eucharist. (*GIL* 30)

They are placed *at the end of* the Liturgy of the Word so that in the light of the readings and homily we can better understand our dependence on God and God's willingness to listen to and answer our prayer. If in practice they are often a little mechanical and perfunctory it is because we Catholics are still not used to formulating and voicing prayers of our own.

An understanding of the structure of the Liturgy of the Word is expected of the reader. If questioned, it is likely that most readers would be able to identify most parts of this section of the Mass. It seems to be a case therefore of bringing to consciousness what we already know.

The GIL explains the closeness of the relationship between the Word of God and the mystery of the eucharist. It points out that from the beginning, the Church came together to read of the actions of Christ and to celebrate the paschal mystery as he instructed.

> For the sacraments are sacraments of faith and faith has its origin and sustenance in the word. The Church is nourished spiritually at the table of God's word and at the table of the eucharist; from the one it grows in wisdom and from the other in holiness. In the Word of God the divine covenant is announced; in the eucharist the new and everlasting covenant is renewed. ... It can never be forgotten, therefore, that the divine word read and proclaimed by the Church in the liturgy has as its one goal the sacrifice of the New Covenant and the banquet of grace, that is, the eucharist. The celebration of Mass in which the word is heard and the eucharist is offered and received forms but one single act of divine worship. (10)

One further point from the GIL should be noted. The document discusses two aids to the proper celebration of the Liturgy of the Word (see 32 – 37). The first is a suitable place reserved for the proclamation of the Word of God – the lectern (This is also referred to by the word *ambo*; lectern is used throughout this handbook because it is the term used in GIL). This is the place from which the readings are to be proclaimed. The second speaks of the books for proclaiming the word of God. It reminds the reader that the Liturgy of the Word must be read from the Lectionary provided for the celebration and not replaced by other pastoral aids such as the Parish Mass Book or a missal.

Conclusion to section on the General Introduction to the Lectionary

What we have learned from this lengthy consideration can be summarised as follows:

> Readers of the Word of God during the liturgy should be qualified and carefully prepared.
> They are expected to have a **biblical formation:** to have developed a love of the Bible and an understanding of the way in which the selections chosen for inclusion in the Lectionary fit together.
> Readers must also have a **liturgical formation**: an understanding of the structure of the Liturgy of the Word and how it relates to the liturgy of the eucharist.

From here, we can turn more purposefully to the question of preparation for the reading we have been assigned. Where it is helpful, specific sections of GIL will be quoted. I acknowledge my debt to Barbara Marian who first suggested this approach to reader preparation in the United States in 1996. I have used it continuously since then and have made such modifications as seem to me to be required for the situation here in Britain.

III. The preparation of the reader - before the ministry begins

A. The Assembled Body of Christ

BEFORE, DURING AND AFTER THE READING, the primary identi–ty of the reader - in fact of everyone engaged in any form of ministry - is as a member of the assembly.

Assembly is a word which has come into use in recent years, and describes *everyone* at the celebration, clergy and laity alike: Christ's people gathered in this place. It is worth noting the importance given to this word in the General Introduction to the Lectionary. Chapter III, which covers Offices and Ministries in the celebration of the Word during Mass, speaks first about the function of the one presiding at the celebration. But its next focus is the *body of the faithful* gathered for the liturgy. The section begins:

Christ's word gathers the people of God as one and increases and sustains them. (44)

The next paragraph states:

In the Liturgy of the Word, the congregation of the faithful still today receives from God the word of his covenant through the faith that comes *by hearing*. ... For their part, the faithful at the celebration of Mass are *to listen* to the Word of God with an inward and outward reverence that will bring them continuous growth in the spiritual life and draw them more deeply into the mystery they celebrate.' (45; emphasis added)

The entire section makes clear that the assembly is expected to come properly disposed to *listen* to the Word of God because they are aware of Christ's presence in the word (see p.12):

it is he who speaks when the holy Scriptures are read in the Church (45; CSL7).

The whole range of 'presences' of Christ is listed in the GIRM: For at the celebration of Mass, which perpetuates the sacrifice of the cross, Christ is really present to the assembly gathered in his name; he is present

in the person of the minister,

in his own word,

and indeed substantially and permanently under the eucharistic elements. (7; 27)

We are used to reverence for the Real Presence of Christ in the Eucharist. We have not yet learned reverence for his Presence in the Word as well, so we don't yet treat it (and thus the ministry of Reader) with the importance it deserves.

Listening

If *listening* to the Word is important, assemblies which use books or missalettes during the Liturgy of the Word should be gently encouraged to think about the implications of following the words in a book. Is this the way we normally listen to someone speaking?

It may be the case that the use of printed aids is their refuge from poor or indifferent reading, or a problem with hearing properly. These issues should be addressed by giving readers proper training in carrying out their ministry better. But, while that is going on, it is important to find a way to suggest that *reading* is not the same as *listening*, that efforts are being made to make listening worthwhile by improving the standard of readers. This won't happen overnight of course, and assemblies must be handled with tact and great diplomacy.

Do *you* know how to listen?

This matter of how the word is listened to has implications for the reader also. What do you do on Sundays when you are not reading? Are *you* listening to the proclamations, or are you too reading the text? You need to listen intently to the Word: firstly, because this is your responsibility as a member of the assembly, and secondly, because by doing so you become a model for receptiveness to the Word.

It may require some self-discipline to become a listener. But the effort of listening to other readers, and judging whether they are successful in conveying the sense of what they are reading, may also help you realise what is involved in being a communicator, and start you thinking of ways you could do it yourself.

This whole matter of the expectations and physical attitude of the assembly during the Liturgy of the Word is a matter of parish catechesis. It needs discussion between readers and parish priest.

B. Basic assumptions about liturgy

There are certain underlying convictions which the reader should have or cultivate as the climate in which preparation is made. We have already started to examine some of these.

The first assumption is that our public worship - our liturgy - matters greatly. Our Sunday celebration is the *source and summit of the Christian life* (CSL10). We come together, not out of a sense of obligation, but because we recognise: that *we have been called* since the time of the apostles to gather on the day of the Lord's resurrection from the tomb; and that *we bring to the celebration* all our hopes and fears, joys, triumphs and failures. We take *from* the celebration the strength given by grace to see us through the week until we return the following Sunday.

The second assumption is that God is present and speaks to his people when holy scriptures are proclaimed in the church.

The third assumption is that good liturgy does not happen by accident - that there is a direct relationship between preparing carefully and worshiping well.

C. Who can be a Reader?

Who can be a reader? Is this a ministry that anyone and everyone can do? Fifteen hundred years ago St Benedict wrote in his

Rule: 'They should not presume to read who by mere chance take up the book... Only those are to discharge these duties who can do so to the edification of the heavens.' The mere wish or willingness to serve as reader does not qualify one for this ministry. The ministry of reading is a charism for the building up of the community. It requires certain obvious qualities such as a good voice. It also requires confidence, maturity, and poise. Further, it also assumes that those who agree to read are of good faith, eager to serve their fellow Christians, and willing to engage in ongoing formation for effective service.

The reader has his/her own proper function in the eucharistic celebration which should be exercised even when there are ministers of higher rank present. (*GIL* 51)

The GIL also recommends that

whenever there is more than one reading, it is better to assign the readings to different readers, if available. (52)

We already know that the first reading (except in Eastertide) is taken from the First or Old Testament while the second reading is drawn from the writings of the apostles. Where the historical period and the perceptions behind the first two readings is very different, this is best brought out by the use of different readers to proclaim them. Also, as will become clear in what follows, there is quite enough work involved in preparing *one* reading well; to give the same attention to two very different selections will be hard work indeed. For this reason, the GIL makes its wise recommendation for two readers. This is the basis of the following suggestions for preparation, the reasons for which will be made clear.

Conclusions about the reader's role

The reader's role is genuinely liturgical.
It is Christ himself who speaks when holy scriptures are read in the church.
This is not a ministry that everyone can do: training and formation are necessary.

IV. Suggestions for improvement

FOLLOWING THE PATTERN USED BY BARBARA MARIAN, the path for the reader is summarised as 4R's - Reflection, Research, Rehearsal, and Review. Each of these is elaborated below.

➤ REFLECTION

• **Begin preparation early** - at least two weeks before the Sunday when you're scheduled to read. This will give time to develop a deeper relationship with the extract, and will also give the confidence that adequate time has been devoted to preparation.

• **Listening and telling.** Before you can present the passage for the hearing of the assembly, you need to hear it yourself.

The best way to do this is to prepare with two or three others, say, those who are preparing the same reading for other Masses on the same weekend, or those who are doing the second reading, or a Bible study group. Take it in turns to listen while one member of the group reads the text. After each reading, take time to consider what word, image or idea is called forth by what you hear. This isn't a time to be concerned about how well you read or to go into detailed analysis of the meaning of the passage: just read as unselfconsciously as possible. After each reading, there should be a pause and then a brief sharing of word, idea or picture. After the last person has read the passage, members of the group should be asked to share with the others so far as they are willing, what the passage says specifically to them - what message they hear for themselves.

What usually results from this listening process is the awareness of how each successive reading calls forth a deeper understanding of the passage. It also ensures that the one assigned to proclaim the reading has heard it several times and has made efforts to find out the meaning of the passage for herself.

This exercise enables us to enter the story with our imaginations, to be present to the story. By doing this - by discovering what we see and how we feel, we make the story our own.

In engaging in this process of listening and telling, we become aware how important it is for us to get it right: it has taken us three readings to reach a meaningful understanding of the passage; the assembly will hear it only once. It will be up to us to have prepared it so well and so carefully that the main point of the passage will be clear.

• **Read the passage aloud many times.** There is an enormous difference between reading to yourself and reading out loud. The most obvious change is one of pace; reading aloud is usually slower than reading to ourselves. Also, we begin to notice the places where the emphasis should fall, where breathing is appropriate.

• **Pray with the text.** Prayer is an extension of the first step - listening and telling - and is an indispensable part of the whole process. What you are doing throughout your preparation is trying to find the meaning of the passage for you. If the reading has no meaning for you, how can you possibly convey meaning to the assembly on Sunday? The way to find the meaning of the passage for you is through prayer.

➤ RESEARCH

While the necessary reflection is going on, the reader needs also to undertake the activities grouped together here under the heading of Research.

• **Check the correct pronunciation** of places and proper names. This is an obvious step, of course, since the presence of unusual names and places is not news. If your presbytery doesn't have a pronunciation guide, you might suggest that this would be a worthwhile investment. If all else fails, you will ask some authoritative

person for help. Once you have the correct pronunciation, practise it until it is as familiar as your own name so that it doesn't let
you down. Say it with confidence over and over so that it holds no
fears for you.

• **Read the passage in its proper context.** This has been partly
covered in the previous chapter under Biblical Formation (page
17). There the first reading for the 13th Sunday in Ordinary Time
in Year A was looked at in its context in the Bible. We saw that
only the first part of the story is given because of its obvious connection with the Gospel of the day. But, in order to proclaim it
well, we need to know the whole of the story - what happened
before and what happened afterwards.

What was the author's intention? How will the story be heard today?

With both the first and second readings, we need to know as
we read the passage what the intention of the author was, so that
our reading has the necessary depth and understanding. To return
to the example of 2 Kings 4:8-11: the First and Second Books of
Kings are classified as Historical Books, the next 'block' of scripture after the first five books of the Bible, the Pentateuch. (See the
outline of Old Testament Books in the Appendix.) Their purpose
is to narrate the complete history of monarchy in Israel's history
and by so doing to help explain to the Jewish people the Exile
which followed. It is the infidelity of the Israelites to the covenant
that brought about the collapse and destruction of Israel and Judah.

> These histories taught Israel what pleases the Lord and what it
> takes to build a new community: obedience and absolute loy-
> alty to the Lord. With God, destruction, punishment, and death
> are never the final word. God's chastisement is always a means
> to an end. If punishment is necessary to open people's eyes,
> then punishment must be seen as an act of God's love. While
> the Books of Kings justify God's actions against sinful Israel
> and Judah, they also do much more for they teach that God is
> merciful and ever willing to offer new opportunities and new

beginnings. *(The Catholic Bible, Personal Study Edition, OUP 1995; p 143)*

This explains not only the author's intention, but also the continuing value of this message for us today.

Before leaving this point, it is worth issuing a caution about trying to apply lessons from the readings to our own times. The authors of the books of the Bible were inspired by God. But they were writing for specific times, specific peoples in cultural circumstances very different from our own. Before we can be confident of understanding what a particular reading means for us, we need to know what it meant to its original hearers. This point is very well developed in the works of J.J.Pilch listed in the bibliography, as well as other works there.

What type of reading is it/what is its literary style?

It is helpful to divide the passages we meet in the Lectionary into three types: narrative readings, what can be called progression of reasoning or arguments, and all other types.

• **Narrative** is the type most often enountered in the first reading - it usually involves telling a story. The important features are the setting in time and place, the characters involved in the story, and the events or happenings. In preparing a narrative passage, it can be very helpful to visualise the scene, to imagine oneself present inside the story, putting in as much detail as seems necessary to bring it to life.

• **Progression of reasoning** is characteristic of most of the second readings which are taken largely from Paul's letters to early Christian communities. They consist of a series of steps in reasoning which lead up to a conclusion. The individual steps need to be presented clearly, which generally means a slower presentation so that the point can register before moving on to the next step. This type of reading also requires a more persuasive presentation as the reader tries to convince the assembly of the truth of the argument and the inescapability of the conclusion.

• **All other types** is a catch-all category which includes such things as poems, songs, exhortations, genealogies, visionary accounts, statements of the law, liturgical instructions, sermons.

The reason for concern with the type of reading is that each requires a different approach and a different style of delivery. As you prepare the passage, you will come to an understanding of the most suitable way to present it, helped by recognising the type of reading it is.

Study the scripture commentaries. This step consists of looking at what others, usually scripture scholars, have to say about the passage you are assigned to read. It comes late in the process because it is more important for you to find out first through prayer and working with others what the passage is saying to you. Only when you have done this should you turn to published commentaries. They may be helpful, they may not, but it isn't a good idea to start with someone else's position before you have worked out your own. The bibliography at the end of the book (p.46) suggests places where commentaries can be found.

These points outline a process we engage in all the time - after we've seen a film, read a book or watched a TV programme. We analyse the story, bringing questions to it and evaluating our response. The value of this process especially where narrative is concerned is that is draws our attention to things we need to know if we are to tell the story well. We begin with a personal awareness that comes from listening to God speaking to us personally. Before we finish, we must hear him speaking to the group - the community of faith that brought us the story, and the community that will hear the story.

➤ REHEARSAL

This section considers those basic skills associated with public speaking, but allied specifically to the ministry of proclaiming the word in the Sunday assembly.

Body language

As we approach the lectern, even before we open our mouths to read, our bodies are sending messages to the assembly about how we feel and our estimation of what we are about to do. We must take care then, that our bodies say the right things.

During the Introductory Rites of the Mass, the reader is usually in the body of the assembly and it is only after the conclusion of the Opening Prayer that s/he comes forward to the ambo (*GIL* 32- 34). This is recommended practice as it makes clear that the readings are being proclaimed by members of the assembly. On the way to the front, the reader's body should be sending the silent message that s/he cares about what is about to happen and so too should the assembly. The pace should be unhurried, infused with the authority of what s/he is about to do, commanding respect and attention.

Once at the ambo, the reader's posture needs strong relaxation to show that s/he wants to be there. But don't confuse relaxation with casualness. Both feet should be planted firmly with the weight resting on both. Hands may be placed on the lectern, but without leaning. This has the advantage of allowing the reader to mark the place without losing it should this be necessary. Relaxation comes from the security of knowing what you are doing and that you have prepared to the best of your ability.

Speed and volume of delivery

These two qualities of public speaking affect each other very strongly and so they are here covered together. To begin with volume: it matters, firstly, if there is amplification at the ambo so that the reader uses a microphone. Rehearsal is essential to make sure that you stand at the correct distance from the microphone, that the so-called 'plosive' consonants (p's and b's) that your voice does carry to all in the congregation. There is a different kind of effort to be made if there is no sound reinforcement in your church. In this case, you need to be able to speak without shouting or strain at a level where all can hear you. Generally, this requires that you take deeper breaths to support greater volume. One way of developing this particular skill is to practise in the church with a friend at the back who will help you find the right level. When the church is full, the sound will be different, so you will need to adjust until you find the balance that is right for you.

Finding the right volume will almost automatically slow down your normal speech rhythms, which is a good thing. *Probably the single-most useful recommendation* for improving the readings in church is simply for the reader to *slow down*. With or without a microphone, you as reader must be aware that the assembly will not be able to understand your proclamation unless you deliver it at a pace which permits it to be taken in and digested. You can help yourself with this matter of pace by taping your reading to see if it is what you want it to be. This is another place where a friend can help by giving you feedback.

Eye contact

In our everyday lives, when we are talking with other people - telling or listening to a story, asking for or giving information - making eye contact is an essential part of our message. Looking at the person/people we're speaking to gives us vital clues about how they are understanding what we are telling them, if the point is getting through. Quite simply, without eye contact, we are deprived of an important element of communication. In spoken communication, eye contact is not just important: it is essential.

This is equally and emphatically true of the proclamations of Scripture during the liturgy. The readings are communication between the reader - the storyteller - and the assembly. No matter how good the preparation, how well-articulated the passage, how well-modulated and beautiful the voice, we are just not doing the job if we keep our heads buried in the Lectionary. As readers, what we are doing is proclaiming the Word and demanding the response of personal involvement from those who are listening. This can only happen when eye contact is made during the proclamation. Another way of putting this is that, without eye contact, the reader gives the impression of reading for herself. By making eye tontact, s/he draws us in and includes us.

In order to do this well, you need to decide while you are preparing the text where the most effective places are to make eye contact and then to practise looking up at these places. In general, eye contact is most effective if it comes at the end of a phrase or sentence. You will need to practise and practise so that the whole delivery package becomes second nature to you. (Be careful of course, not to make eye contact with phrases that begin: 'Woe betide those sinners...!')

It is very helpful to make a photocopy of the page in the lectionary where your reading is found. Mark your copy during your preparation with the places where you need to breathe, underline the words you want to emphasise, mark and memorise the phrases where you want to make eye contact. Then on the day of your reading, the text open before you in the lectionary will hold no terrors and will be like the face of an old friend. Remember though that on the day, you must read only from the Lectionary (GIL 35)

When you first begin making eye contact, you may find that no one is looking. This is especially the case if your church uses mass books or missalettes and the assembly has got into the habit of reading for themselves during the proclamations. Don't be discouraged: the better your reading gets, the more confident the assembly will become with it and the less they will be tempted to look at something else. We have already covered the importance of helping the assembly to see that their responsibility during the Liturgy of the Word is to listen attentively (see pp. 27-28 above).

On the day

Let's put it all together this far and run through what we do as readers during the Mass on the day we are scheduled to read. The priest closes the Introductory Rites with the Closing Prayer to which the assembly responds 'Amen'. While they are sitting down, the reader goes forward to the lectern, up the central aisle with purpose, but not hurrying, bowing to the altar, and arriving at the lectern before the Lectionary. After a quick glance to make sure the book is open at the right page, the reader looks up and gathers the community with her eyes and, when all is quiet, says while still looking at the people 'A reading from the second book of Kings'. (We do not say 'first' or 'second' reading following GIL 121 which states that words printed in the Lectionary to identify passages are not spoken because it is already clear from practice what the item is – in the same way, if there is no cantor, there is no need to say 'The Responsorial Psalm is...', but simply to proclaim the response which the assembly is called upon to repeat.)

Silence - and a warning

Having completed the passage, there is the need for silence. To repeat what GIL says about this:

> The dialogue between God and his people taking place through the Holy Spirit demands short intervals of silence, suited to the assembly, as an opportunity to take the Word of God to heart and to prepare a response to it in prayer. (28)

The length of the silence after the readings is probably best placed under the control of the reader. Reaching the end of the passage, the reader can step back slightly, lower her head in meditation for a time depending on what the assembly gets accustomed to, before moving forward again, raising her head and saying 'This is the word of the Lord'.

A word of warning. Don't make this change unless it has been discussed and agreed with the parish priest and other readers, and the community has been advised to expect it. Otherwise, people are likely to think you've forgotten what to do next or had a seizure. The approach to change will be repeated at the end of this section (page 42).

Get help: ask a friend to listen critically. Tape or videotape yourself reading. The first part of this recommendation has already been made. The suggestion that you use a video is not essential and is perhaps only for the very brave, but it is the only way for you to know what the assembly sees and hears when you proclaim the Word.

On the day of reading

• **Get to church** 15 to 20 minutes early. This gives you time to settle and assures those in charge of the liturgy that you are present and no replacement is needed.

• **Check** the lectionary and microphone. Be sure the book is open at the correct place. If the Lectionary is carried in the entrance procession, make sure the marker is in the right place. If there is an entrance procession and you're the person carrying the book, open it to the right place when you reach the ambo.

• **Allow time** to recall the main point(s) of the reading.

• **Put yourself** in the care of the Holy Spirit.

• **Join wholeheartedly** in the liturgy. Be present for the whole of the celebration, not just the part you are reading.

➤ REVIEW

• **Evaluate** your interpretations and delivery. Some time after you have given your reading, think about how you did - whether the understanding you had at the time continues to feel right, or whether there is an aspect that didn't occur to you until later. Consider whether the way you delivered the proclamation could be improved; if so, what could be changed. What will you do differently next time?

• **Get a trusted friend** to give feedback.

This needs to be someone whose opinion you value, whom you trust to tell you what may not always be comfortable to hear, who, while remaining your friend, will tell you clearly what can be improved.

Summary of Suggestions for Improvement

Opposite is a complete list of all the suggestions that have been made:

REFLECTION
1. Begin preparation early – 10 days/2 weeks
2. Listening and telling:
   Work with one or more partners to bring the readings to life.
3. Read the passage aloud many times
4. Pray with the text: find its meaning for YOU.

RESEARCH
5. Check correct pronunciation of place/proper names.
6. Read the passage in its proper context in the Scriptures.
7. Study scripture commentaries.
8. Find answers to the following questions:
   — What was the author's intention?
   — What is the literary style?
   — What are the realities of the original community? What are the differences between our ancestors and ourselves in the way the story will be heard?

REHEARSAL
9. Take into account basic communication skills:
   — Body language
   — Volume and speed of delivery
   — Eye contact
10. Get help: ask a friend to listen critically.
    Tape/videotape yourself reading.

FINAL PREPARATION ON DAY OF READING
• Get to church 15-20 minutes early.
• Check lectionary and microphone.
• Allow time to recall main point of reading.
• Put yourself in the care of the Holy Spirit.
• Join wholeheartedly in the liturgy.

REVIEW
11. Evaluate your interpretations and delivery.
12. Get a trusted friend to provide critique.

Final remarks about preparation

God speaks through the dialogue of storyteller and listener, through proclamation and acclamation.

Readers are only one part of this dialogue and not the most important part - which is listening.

Learning to be a good storyteller is not something that can be learned just by reading a text. It requires lots of practice in telling and in listening to the story.

It is not only helpful, there is a real need for readers to meet regularly as a group – to encourage one another and build morale, to provide opportunities for listening and telling. The frequency of such meetings will depend on local circumstances: once a month to consider the readings of four Sundays at a time is good. In addition, a meeting at the beginning of each liturgical season is helpful to discuss the flavour of the season which is reflected in the readings. These seasonal meetings will be even more useful if they include others – those involved in planning the liturgy, musicians, catechists, greeters, and anyone else who is interested. And, of course, the parish priest.

Readers need to be on their feet often – at least once a month is desirable. This is especially the case if the recommendation can be followed that there be two readers for each Sunday. If your church has more readers than will fit this recommendation, perhaps some consideration should be given to commissioning readers for a fixed period (say, three years as is the case with Extraordinary Ministers of the Eucharist) and retiring them on a rota at the end of this period to make room if it is needed. But the situation of reading only two or three times a year because the list is so long is not a happy one – no one gets a chance to develop any real experience of this ministry or to get comfortable with its demands.

Warning again

Health warning! If you've read this far and want to use the suggestions to improve the way you proclaim the scriptures, you need to be aware that unexplained changes will almost certainly lead to resistance.

The things you can do to improve the speed and volume of delivery, eye contact and body language are within your control: begin working with these.

But the other aspects, particularly the introduction of silence after the reading, the use of two readers - one for the first and one for the second reading - the way in which the body of readers as a whole prepare: these are things that need time to consider, to work on, to agree on, and to present to the assembly in a way they will understand and accept. This might not happen quickly, but don't lose heart - good ideas have a long lead-time. We are part of a tradition that stretches back more than two thousand years. Given this time-scale, twenty more minutes' wait isn't going to hurt.

The role of the parish priest

Throughout all the recommendations contained in this handbook, there is the implicit understanding which must now be made explicit: that the parish priest has overall responsibility for the celebration of the Liturgy of the Word. For this reason, he is a vital member of the group that wishes to improve the way Scripture is proclaimed and needs to be consulted throughout. The General Introduction to the Lectionary makes all of this clear by saying about the presider:

> Personally or through others he sees to it that the word of God is properly proclaimed. He then as a rule reserves to himself the task of composing comments to help the people to listen more attentively and to preach a homily that fosters in them a richer understanding of the word of God. (38)

This means that his presence would be very desirable during the listening and telling, during the research, during the sharing among readers as they look for the meaning of the passages in the lives of those who first heard the passage and in their lives.

If the readers are ready to introduce the change but the assembly is not quite sure, one thing that might be worth trying is to ask them for a fixed period - say Advent or Lent or the next six Sundays - to try the new situation, refraining from comment until the end of this period. Whether it succeeds is mainly up to the quality of the preparation that the readers put in so that the proclamations can do their work.

As Isaiah tells us in the fifth reading of the Easter Vigil,

Yes, as the rain and the snow come down from the heavens and do not return without watering the earth, making it yield and giving growth to provide seed for the sower and bread for the eating, so the Word that goes from my mouth does not return to me empty, without carrying out my will and succeeding in what it was sent to do. (Is 55: 11)

What an awesome responsibility it is for us, as readers, to be part of this process!

V. The Spiritual Dimension
of Ministry

S O FAR, THIS HANDBOOK HAS BEEN MAINLY CONCERNED with what might be called the technical aspects of the ministry of the word. However, before we go, there is something further to be said about what the proper discharge of our ministry will lead do - the effect it should have on us.

If we do our work as ministers of the word with the attention and focus described in preceding paragraphs, how can we not be changed by it? Such attention to the Word of God, spoken to us and listened to so that we can act as channels of God's message to his people - this is bound to lead us closer to God.

A way of life

In choosing ministry, we must realise that we are choosing not just a way of serving our community, but a way of life. True, we are committed to this way of life by our baptism which summons all of us to be Christ in the world, but by putting ourselves at the service of others at prayer through proclaiming the Word, we can no longer keep this choice on the back burner.

In the preparation outlined above, one of the first things we do is open ourselves to the power of the Spirit working in us as we listen to hear the word. This openness and listening becomes part of our prayer which is the foundation of our ministry.

Then, having heard the Word of God, having proclaimed it to

the best of our ability, it takes root within us and we have to do something about it. At the Sunday celebration, together with other members of the body of Christ, we respond to the word with prayer and song before the breaking of bread and the offering of wine as a memorial of Christ's death and resurrection. Then, after sharing in communion, the assembly is sent forth to be Christ in the world, to continue his work in bringing all people to him. This is the lay ministry to which we are all called - to be living examples of faith, to embrace discipleship as a way of life. Our closeness to the word makes this vocation inescapable.

In closing, may I wish you joy in being a channel for bringing the Word of God to your community. May God's blessings be on you and on your community through the exercise of your ministry. May you be a holy person doing holy work.

BIBLIOGRAPHY

This is not a scholarly bibliography: the list of books given here is the result of one person's experience of materials gathered over a number of years which have proved helpful. It is not meant to be exhaustive, merely suggestive. Where it seemed to be helpful, an annotation is given to provide more detailed information and a personal recommendation.

Documents and Texts

Flannery, Austin, OP, editor, POST CONCILIAR DOCUMENTS OF VATICAN COUNCIL II, Volume II, The Liturgical Press, Collegeville, Minnesota, 1982. Contains The General Introduction to the Lectionary.

Keifer, Ralph A, TO HEAR AND PROCLAIM: Introduction to the Lectionary for Mass, (with commentary for Musicians and Priests), National Association of Pastoral Musicians, Washington, DC, 1983 (distributed in UK by Decani Music). The advantage of this publication is that it is a single-volume copy of the Introduction.

THE LITURGY DOCUMENTS: A Parish Resource, Liturgy Training Publications, 1991. This contains in one volume seven of the Roman Documents including those most important to liturgy planners and readers in the parish: The Constitution on the Sacred Liturgy, The General Instruction of the Roman Missal, the Lectionary for Mass: Introduction. Each document is preceded by a useful overview and outline making this a very easy reference to use.

THE BIBLE DOCUMENTS: A Parish Resource, Liturgy Training Publications, 2001. This contains all of the church's most important documents on the scriptures including The Lectionary for Mass: Introduction, and is a companion publication to the Liturgy Documents. A useful reference work to have available in the parish.

The *General Instruction on the Roman Missal* was issued in a revised version (third edition) in 2000. An English translation was in preparation at the time of printing. The second edition is to be found in *The Liturgy Documents* (above).

Useful Reference Materials

A. General information

Bonneau, Normand, OMI, PREPARING THE TABLE OF THE WORD, Novalis: The Liturgical Press, 1997.

Connell, Martin, GUIDE TO THE REVISED LECTIONARY, Liturgy Training Publications, 1998.

Charpentier, Etienne, HOW TO READ THE OLD TESTAMENT, SCM Press Ltd., 1982.

Charpentier, Etienne, HOW TO READ THE NEW TESTAMENT, SCM Press Ltd., 1982.

Newland, Mary Reed, A POPULAR GUIDE THROUGH THE OLD TESTAMENT, St Mary's Press, Winona, Minnesota, 1999.

Pilch, John J, THE CULTURAL DICTIONARY OF THE BIBLE, The Liturgical Press, Collegeville, Minnesota, 1999.

Pilch, John J, THE CULTURAL WORLD OF THE APOSTLES, Year A (others to follow), The Liturgical Press, 2001.

Pilch, John J, THE CULTURAL WORLD OF JESUS, for Year A, Year B and Year C, The Liturgical Press, Collegeville, Minnesota, 1995, 1996, and 1997.

Hiesberger, Jean Marie, General Editor, THE CATHOLIC BIBLE: Personal Study Edition, OUP, 1995. I have found this the most useful personal guide: it is divided into two parts. The first section gives reading guides for each book of the Bible. In addition, this part provides such helpful information as who the main players are, what the reader should look out for, when and where the action took place, why the book was written, who the author was, and a summary of the story. Each chapter in the first part concludes with questions for reflection or discussion. The second part consists of the texts of the Old Testament and the New Testament of the New American Bible. This would be a good investment for the committed reader.

Newsom, Carol A and Sharon H Ringe (Editors), THE WOMEN's BIBLE COMMENTARY, SPCK, 1992. This volume does for all the books of the Bible something similar to what the Pilch books do – it provides an understanding of the cultural background, but with special attention to the role of women, especially in Old Testament times and gives a dimension to the readings that might otherwise be missing.

B. Commentaries on the Sunday readings

Brief commentaries, especially for those new to this aspect of preparation

THE LITURGY PLANNER, edited by Stephen Dean, published by Decani Music three times a year with an Autumn Extra. This periodical provides music and liturgy suggestions for the season, including for each Sunday a section entitled Hear the Word which is a brief commentary on that day's readings.

MUSIC AND LITURGY-LITURGY PLANNER, commentaries by Patrick Geary and printed as part of the periodical Music & Liturgy, the journal of The Society of Saint Gregory. In addition to suggestions for music, the commentary for each Sunday also contains Thoughts on the Day which comments on the readings assigned for that day.

Frank J Mulligan, READING AT MASS: Guidelines for the Lector, The Liturgical Press, Collegeville, Minnesota, 1990.

More commentaries with suggestions

Peter J Scagnelli, SOURCEBOOK FOR SUNDAYS AND SEASONS: An Almanac of Parish Liturgy, Liturgy Training Publications, 2001. This Sourcebook is published every year and is of use to all who minister during the Sunday Mass, not just readers. This is an invaluable parish resource as liturgy groups will find the seasonal overviews and explanations very helpful, while readers will benefit as a group from the Lectionary Overview. After the general information at the beginning of the book, there is a season-by-season section before a calendar which looks at each day's Mass.

WORKBOOK FOR LECTORS AND GOSPEL READERS, published each year by Liturgy Training Publications. Although aimed at the churches in the United States and Canada which use different lectionaries, nevertheless, this is a very useful guide that is aimed at people who are not biblical scholars. There is the added benefit of a pronunciation guide for unusual names. A Workbook for the Triduum is published as a separate booklet since the readings are always the same.

More advanced commentaries

Brown, Raymond E. et al, editors, THE NEW JEROME BIBLICAL COMMENTARY, Geoffrey Chapman, 1989.

DAYS OF THE LORD: The Liturgical Year, 7 volumes, The Liturgical Press, Collegeville, Minnesota, 1994.

Dianne Bergant, CSA, editor, THE COLLEGEVILLE BIBLE COMMENTARY: OLD TESTAMENT, The Liturgical Press, 1992.

Robert Karris, OFM, editor, THE COLLEGEVILLE BIBLE COMMEN-TARY: NEW TESTAMENT, The Liturgical Press, 1992.

John L Mc Kenzie, SJ, *Dictionary of the Bible,* Simon & Schuster, 1995. (This book has just gone out of print, but is probably still obtainable second-hand.)

C. Technical Skills: Public Speaking

There are numerous books on public speaking skills which could be consulted. The two listed below cover the same ground, but with specific attention being paid to the demands of proclaiming the scriptures. They are recommended because of the particular attention they pay to the church environment and their use of Scriptural texts for examples and exercises.

Lonergan, Ray, A WORKBOOK FOR LECTORS: A Well-trained tongue, Liturgy Training Publications, 1982.

Rosser, Aelred R, A WELL-TRAINED TONGUE: Formation in the Ministry of Reader, Liturgy Training Publications, 1996.

A BRIEF GUIDE TO THE OLD TESTAMENT

Because they were written by many authors over a long period of time, the stories in the books of the Old Testament can sometimes seem very far from our own situations and difficult to understand. It is worth reminding ourselves that despite appearances, the Old Testament is just one story of the people of God, our ancestors in faith, and the way in which they learned about God through the events of their lives. The following brief summary is given to help clarify the shape of this story.

The Pentateuch:

The Books of Genesis, Exodus, Leviticus, Numbers and Deuteronomy.

The name Pentateuch means a five-part writing – one book in five volumes. They are called Torah in Jewish tradition which means it contains the basic teachings of the Jewish faith. Tradition assigns authorship to Moses but scholars agree they were written by several authors and attained their present form over the course of centuries.

The Historical Books:

The Books of Joshua, Judges, Ruth, 1 Samuel and 2 Samuel, 1 Kings and 2 Kings.

These seven books are called the 'Deuteronomistic History' because the Book of Deuteronomy serves as a kind of preface to the whole collection and includes some of the books in the next section as well. The writers of these books have taken many stories and combined them to explain why the nation collapsed and why the people were led into exile. They wanted to communicate a simple message to their audience: Learn from the past.

The Chronicler's History and the Later Histories

The Books of 1 Chronicles and 2 Chronicles, Ezra and Nehemiah, Tobit, Judith, Esther, 1 Maccabees, 2 Maccabees.

Scholars identify the chronicler's history as one of the three major units telling the story of the Israelite people. Like the deuteronomistic history outlined in the section above, the chronicler's history tells the story of the Israelite kingdoms and their fall. But while the deuteronomic history tries to explain why they fell, the chronicler's real purpose is to outline the prospects for Israel's future.

The Wisdom Books[1]

The Books of Job, Psalms, Proverbs, Ecclesiastes, Song of Songs, Wisdom, Sirach (Ecclesiasticus).

These books answer a new kind of question: what kind of role does God play in everyday life? The answers in no way contributed to what we have come to know as 'salvation history'. Instead, they form a 'guide for successful living' which had universal appeal.

Job: a dramatic poem that treats the problem of suffering of the innocent, and of retribution.

Psalms: a collection of religious songs under the major headings of hymns, laments, and songs of thanksgiving.

Proverbs: an anthology of mostly short sayings in poetical form whose purpose is to teach wisdom for successful living.

Ecclesiastes: a treatise on the vanity, or emptiness, of all things. The book is concerned with the purpose and value of human life.

---

1 The summary of this section is taken from The Catholic Bible (further details in the bibliography)

The Song of Songs: a collection of love poems full of sensuous imagery. It could be seen as a portrayal of ideal human love.

Wisdom: oratory from the Jewish community of Alexandria about one hundred years before the coming of Christ, the author explaining traditions and themes familiar to Judaism but reinterpreting them from the experience of living in a Hellenistic culture.

Sirach: a collection of proverbs dealing with moral instruction, written to show that real wisdom was to be found in the traditions of Israel and not in the godless philosophy of the day.

The Prophets:

1. The Books of Isaiah, Jeremiah, Lamentations, Baruch, Ezekiel, Daniel.

Like many books of the Bible, this collection was written much later than the period to which they refer. But they follow a similar pattern. First the prophet experiences life within a believing faith community which nourishes the prophet's relationship and growing intimacy with God. Sometime during the prophet's life, God is experienced more profoundly to the extent that the prophet feels called to delve into the whole mystery of God as it relates to the community. He develops an acute sensitivity to violations of justice, especially to the poor and rejected. The prophet feels compelled to call these incidents to the attention of the community, often with warnings of what will happen if the community does not change. The prophet's message is not always one of doom. He continually reminds the people of God's faithful love. God's love and peace will be manifest if the people attend to the concerns of the poor and to the works of justice.

2. The Twelve Minor Prophets:

The Books of Hosea, Joel, Amos, Obadiah, Jonah, Micah, Nahum, Habakkuk, Zephaniah, Haggai, Zechariah, Malachi.

The authors of this collection (referred to as the Book of the

Twelve) are called minor because their writings are short in comparison with the major prophets – Isaiah, Jeremiah, Ezekiel and Daniel. Each of the authors wrote to deal with a specific situation of their own time, but there is a pattern to the content of the books which is more or less observable in each of the works: sin followed by judgment followed by salvation or the promise of restoration. Taken as a whole, these books are both a reflection on the past and a lesson for the future. Those who edited the prophetic books were heavily influenced by the theology of Deuteronomy: Sin does not go unpunished, but God is ultimately merciful and wants only the repentance and restoration of Israel. This call to repentance is heard throughout this collection.

A Suggested Training Course for Readers

Introduction

It is unlikely that any parish wishing to introduce a training course and commissioning of its readers will be starting from scratch. This means there will probably already be a group of readers who have been involved in this ministry for various periods of time, probably without any sustained training. The question is: where to begin? It will be essential to persuade people who have been doing something different that there is a need to change and that there is an authoritative source which gives clear guidelines about the expectations of the reader. There are also great benefits to be gained from having all readers undergo the training together – this helps develop a shared understanding of the ministry which will strengthen the conduct of the liturgy.

Preliminary meeting

Parishes might like to consider inviting all readers already serving on the rota and any prospective readers to attend a Preliminary Meeting when the importance of the role of readers and the guidelines contained in the General Introduction to the Liturgy can be presented and discussed. Then, a training course could begin with the understanding that the course will finish with a commissioning of those who have undergone the training; after this, only commissioned readers will be used. Readers could be commissioned for a period of three years, with perhaps a renewal of their promises of commitment in the intervening years.

Advent

Appropriate timing for the running of the course is the beginning of the liturgical year – Advent – when we remind ourselves of the coming of the Word. The commissioning could then be scheduled for a Sunday Mass during the Christmas season.

Involve the whole Assembly

While the readers are undergoing training, it will be helpful for the parish priest to use some time in the same period to catechise the assembly about what is happening during the Liturgy of the Word and what the role of the assembly is. The weekly Sunday bulletin can also carry the same information. In this way, the whole assembly can progress to a better understanding of and love for the Word of God in the Sunday celebration.

Training Course: Content

Introduction

Why this course is needed

Biblical Formation

Introduction to the Old Testament
Introduction to the New Testament
How the Lectionary has been compiled
Useful resources

Liturgical Formation

Meaning of the Liturgy of the Word
Structure of the Liturgy of the Word
Ministers involved and expectations of them
Relationship to the Liturgy of the Eucharist
Useful resources

Technical/public speaking skills

Speed and volume of delivery
Movement/body language
Eye contact
Useful resources

Evaluation and plan for future

Training Course: Suggested Timetable

Preliminary meeting

Importance of the Liturgy of the Word and the guidelines
contained in the General Introduction to the Lectionary

WEEK ONE

Introduction: overall plan and aims for first session
Ministry in the Church: the role of the reader
Biblical formation: Old Testament
Skill training: Reflection
Listening and telling
Summary

WEEK TWO

Introduction: aims for second session
Biblical formation: New Testament
Skill training: Research
Summary

WEEK THREE

Introduction: aim for third session
Liturgical Formation: structure
Ministers involved and expectations of them
Skill Formation: Rehearsal
Public speaking skills
Summary

WEEK FOUR

Introduction: aim for final session
Liturgical Formation: How the Liturgy of the Word
        relates to the Liturgy of the Eucharist
Skill formation: Rehearsal
Summary and conclusion

COMMISSIONING OF READERS

The commissioning of readers usually takes place during the celebration of Mass on a Sunday after the period of training outlined above. The form which follows is one way in which commissioning can be done,[1]

Introduction

> *1827. The word of God, as proclaimed in the sacred Scripture, lies at the heart of our Christian life and is integral to all our liturgical celebrations.*
>
> *1828. This order is not intended for the institution of readers by the bishop, who uses the rite contained in the Roman Pontifical. Rather, this blessing is for parish readers who have the responsibility of proclaiming the Scriptures at Mass and other liturgical services. Care should be taken to see that readers are properly prepared for the exercise of their ministry before receiving this blessing. The functions of the reader are given in no. 66 of the General Instruction of the Roman Missal.*
>
> *1829. If desired, each new reader may be presented with a lectionary or bible after the prayer of blessing.*
>
> *1830. This blessing is given by the pastor, who may also delegate it to another priest or a deacon.*

ORDER OF BLESSING WITHIN MASS

> *After the gospel reading and the homily, the celebrant will usually begin by talking about this ministry, commending the readers for the diligence of their preparation, and reminding the ministers and the assembled people of the parish of its significance. He then presents to the people whose who are to be commissioned, using these or similar words:*

Our brothers and sisters N. and N. are to be commissioned as Readers during liturgical celebrations.

---

[1] adapted from Book of Blessings of the Roman Rite, Prepared by ICEL, published by Catholic Book Publishing Co., New York: 1989.

The priest pauses as the named ministers come forward to stand in front of him. He then addresses the new ministers:

> In this ministry you must be examples of Christian living in faith and conduct; your continuing study of the sacred Scriptures will bring you ever closer to an understanding of God's enduring love for his people and his plan for our salvation.

The priest then asks the ministers the following questions:

Priest: Are you resolved to undertake the office of Proclaimer of the Word for the service and growth of the church?

Response: **I am.**

Priest: Are you resolved to proclaim the Word of Sacred Scripture withthe utmost respect and care?

Response: **I am.**

Priest: Are you resolved to continue to study and pray with others to deepen your understanding of the Word and your ability toproclaim it well?

Response: **I am.**

Priest: Are you resolved to strive more earnestly to live the Christian life, to give good example and through an increasing knowledge and love of Sacred Scripture, to take your faithmore seriously?

Response: **I am.**

General Intercessions

The celebrant says:

> The word of God calls us out of darkness into the light of faith. With the confidence of God's children let us ask the Lord to hear our prayers and to bless these readers:

59

Response: **Lord, hear our prayer.**
Or: **Lord, graciously hear us.**

Assisting minister:

For the Church, that we may continue to respond to
the word of God which is proclaimed in our midst . . .
Lord, hear us [*or* We pray to the Lord]. *Response.*

For all who listen as the Scriptures are proclaimed, that
God's word may find in them a fruitful field . . .
Lord, hear us. *Response.*

For those who have not heard the message of Christ,
that we may be willing to bring them the good news
of salvation . . .
Lord, hear us. *Response.*

For our readers, that they will continue to
study and pray
so that with deep faith and confident voice
they may announce God's saving words . . .
Lord, hear us. *Response.*

Prayer of Blessing

With hands extended over the new readers, the celebrant says:

Everlasting God,
when he read in the synagogue at Nazareth,
your Son proclaimed the good news of salvation
for which he would give up his life.

Bless these readers.
As they proclaim your words of life,
strengthen their faith
that they may read with conviction and boldness,
and put into practice what they read.

We ask this through Christ our Lord.

Amen.